THE LANGUAGE OF

CHOICE THEORY

THE LANGUAGE OF
CHOICE THEORY

WILLIAM GLASSER, M.D., AND CARLEEN GLASSER, M.ED.

HarperPerennial
A Division of HarperCollins*Publishers*

HarperCollins books may be purchased for educational, business, or sales promotional use. For information please write: Special Markets Department, HarperCollins Publishers, Inc., 10 East 53rd Street, New York, NY 10022.

FIRST EDITION

Designed by Nancy Singer Olaguera

Glasser, William, 1925–
      The language of choice theory / William Glasser and Carleen Glasser.—1st. ed.
          p. cm.
      ISBN 0-06-095323-3
      1. Interpersonal communication. 2. Interpersonal relations.
I. Glasser, Carleen. II. Title
BF637.C45G57 1999
158.2—DC21

99 00 01 02 03 HC/❖ 10 9 8 7 6 5 4 3 2 1

CONTENTS

INTRODUCTION

The external control psychology that we use when we have difficulty getting along with others is destructive to the relationships all of us need. In my 1998 book, *Choice Theory: A New Psychology of Personal Freedom*, I offer a new psychology that is the diametric opposite of external control. The more it is used, the more it improves our relationships.

In that book I propose that we give up external control psychology completely and replace it with choice theory to enable us to do something we have failed to do since history began: significantly improve the way we get along with one another. Doing this would result in better marriages, happier families, more successful schools, and increased quality and productivity in the workplace.

Since the best way to understand theory is through its practice, this book examines the bossy or controlling language we use when we can't get along with one another. Specifically, we use the language associated with criticizing, blaming, complaining, threatening, punishing, and/or rewarding to try to get what we want. This external control language always harms and often destroys the relationships we must have for happiness and success. External control is a plague on all humanity.

Choice theory is exactly the opposite. Its language, never bossy or controlling, is always an attempt to work out the differences between people in a way that satisfies both parties. For example, open, fair, and noncoercive negotiation is always the choice of people who use this new theory. They will listen, support, sustain, tolerate, and be patient with one another.

The difference between the two languages is startling. External control speech is peppered with the imperative tense, with *should*, *must*, and *have to*, plus threats of punishment if you don't do what you're told and promises of reward if you do. Choice theory language helps us to work out problems with one another; external control language increases them.

In the following pages this new way of expressing ourselves will be clearly seen in four situations. In love and marriage, where both parties should be working to keep the power in the relationship reasonably close to equal, external control language will quickly and permanently destroy the balance of power that is necessary if the couple is to have any chance for happiness. In marriage, the most difficult relationship for people to walk away from, the language will escalate to cursing, nagging, scolding, henpecking, arguing, and withdrawing. No marriage can long withstand such an onslaught.

In parent-child, teacher-student, manager-worker relationships, in which the power is almost always in the hands of the parent, teacher, or manager, the parties should work to give children, students, and workers more power than they usually have in the external control world we live in. The more power the parent, teacher, or manager gives, the more chance each has to achieve his or her goals.

Choice theory language is based on the belief that the only person whose behavior each of us can control is ourself. All we can give and receive from others is information. But information by itself can't make us do anything. Each of us—even in the face of a severe threat, if we are willing to suffer the consequences—can choose what we do. And no matter how we are threatened, no one can make us think the way they want.

Finally, the main difference between external control language and the choice theory alternative is creativity. Without some creativity, any close relationship will grow stale. All people are capable of creativity, but both the language and thought processes of people who rely on external control is almost totally noncreative. It is stereotypical, made up mostly of a few overused words and threats. In contrast, choice theory language is rich with creative, caring words, never any threats.

As much as most people appreciate finding creative ways to deal with their relationships, they do not realize how their use of external control language keeps them in a noncreative rut. This book will introduce you to a new way to talk with people and, in a sense, a more creative way to live your life. Even a creative insult is preferable to the ubiquitous "f—— you," the least creative expression in any language.

As you face the open book, the examples of external control language are on the left-hand pages. Opposite, on the right, are examples of how choice theory language would be used in the same situation. Remember, choice theory language is new, and your first impulse may be to say: *It won't work, it's too permissive,* or *I'm afraid I'll lose control. Coercion and punishment are quicker and better.* And in fact, for a *short time* in some situations in which you have a lot of power, external control language may seem to work. But in the long run, it never does and never will. The misery of accepting external control is too high a price for most of us to pay.

After you read a few pages you may want to cover up the right-hand page and try to create your own choice theory alternative before you look at ours. It's good practice; ours are hardly the only choices. Guide yourself by thinking: *If someone said that to me, would I feel as close to that person as I do now?*

Keep in mind that the relationships we need are rarely short term. The effect of external control is cumulative; in rearing children it may seem to surface suddenly in adolescence. But it's not sudden. External control is always resisted, and over time this resistance builds and finally erupts, making what was initially a small problem more difficult—often impossible—to solve. With external control you may win a few battles but you always lose the war.

THE LANGUAGE OF

CHOICE THEORY

PARENT TO CHILD

How many times do I have to tell you? Bedtime is nine o'clock! No television tomorrow night if you don't go right to bed this minute.

As long as you're quiet and don't disturb anyone, you can go to bed when you get sleepy. But before *I* get too sleepy, would you like me to read you a story?

Get off that phone right now! I'm serious. I'm just about ready to stop letting you use the phone at all after dinner.

Things with the phone just aren't working out. No one can get through. Grandma said she tried for three hours last night. I'm willing to put in call-waiting, but when someone calls I need you to get right off. Can we try that?

Your room's a pigpen. Clean it up or no car this weekend.

Look, I'm at the point where all I want is for you to keep your door closed. But I have to be honest: I'd like you to clean up your room; it bothers me. If you want some help from me, ask and I'll be glad to pitch in. But I'm not going to clean it for you anymore.

Do your homework now. I don't care what it is. You have to do it or no TV tonight.

Okay, I'm not going to argue with you. Let's look that homework over together to see if you understand it. And I'll be right here to help you if you get stuck.

If I catch you anywhere near those kids again, you're grounded for life. All they ever do is get into trouble.

I'm frightened at the idea of you being out alone with those kids at your age. It's okay if you see them here when I'm home. If I get to know them a little better, I may change my mind. But if you have a better idea, I'll listen. As long as we keep talking, it'll be okay.

You wanted the dog. Well, I'll tell you, I'm sick and tired of walking her. She's going to the pound if you don't start taking better care of her.

Look, we've got the dog. I love her, and I'm not going to get rid of her. But I'm tired of being the only one who walks her. And I'm tired of asking you and being told, "I'll do it later." The dog needs some care. How can we work this problem out?

If you don't stop fighting over the TV, Dad and I are going to shut it off for a week.

How about this? When we get the TV guide on Sunday, we'll go through it together. We'll each get a choice, and we'll rotate who goes first to keep it fair. This way the worst that can happen is that we'll only have to fight over the TV once a week.

Over my dead body, you'll quit school at sixteen!

Talk to the school. I think you have to have a full-time job to quit. You're surprised I'm not putting up a fight? Look, I won't even put up a fight if you decide to go back.

Are you crazy? No child of mine will ever get her nose pierced.

Get anything pierced you want. My love doesn't depend on what you look like. But don't do it until I get a good picture of you the way you are.

You did it once without a condom! You're pregnant and now you're seeking excuses for it! My advice is to pack your things and go live with his family. Maybe his mother wants a grandchild. I don't.

Tell me what you want, and I'll do everything I can to help you. We're talking about your life and a new life here. This requires some serious thinking and a lot of talking. But I'm not going to stop loving you, if that's what you're worried about.

Forget it, you're not getting a car. I don't care if you're working, you need that money for college.

This is a tough one for me. I know how you feel. And I know you've been working hard. I want to do what's right, but I don't know what's right. Would you be willing to find out what a car costs—insurance, gas, and everything? There's a lot more to getting a car than you realize. Make it a research project, and I'll listen to how you're going to cover all the expenses. I won't always agree with you, but I'll listen.

You think you're gay? My God, do you want to kill us? There are no queers in our family. Get out!

All we can tell you is we love you. Please talk to us, you must have a lot on your mind. We're happy you felt free to come to us. There must be support groups for parents in our situation. We'll look into it, and if you hear of anything let us know. If you want, we'll all go together.

If that's what you want to wear, forget about shopping with me. I won't spend my hard-earned money on those ridiculous clothes.

Well, if these clothes are in the store, I guess people buy them. I won't stop you from buying this outfit, but let's look and see if we can find some stuff that looks better on you. We've got time. It's fun going shopping with you.

LOVE AND MARRIAGE

You can't wear a sport shirt to an affair like this! You'll look like a bum and embarrass me. You've got to wear a shirt and tie.

Honey, I know you hate being uncomfortable, but this affair is pretty formal. How about wearing that new tie you picked out to go with the navy suit? You look great in it.

You never feel like sex anymore. I'm tired of asking for it. What's your problem?

Honey, we hardly ever make love anymore, but I don't think the problem is sex. We could do it as well as we ever did if we wanted to. I think it has to do with how we've been treating each other. Most of the time we don't really talk and when we do, it's to complain or blame. And I'm willing to admit that I've been doing a lot of the blaming. How's that going to get us back to where we used to be?

It was your idea that I stay home with the kids. And now all I hear is that we don't have enough money for anything I want. I didn't want that new minivan; I wanted a car. When do I get some of the things I want?

I don't know what to do. I need things. And I want a few things I don't need. You tell me we don't have the money, so I nag. I hate it as much as you do. What else can I do? Maybe there isn't any more to this marriage than what we have. I don't know. But I'll tell you, I'm willing to try for more. I still love you. What are you willing to do?

Till death do us part, and I keep thinking I must be dead. Maybe we shouldn't have gotten married. I'm miserable. Why are you doing this to me?

I don't know what's gone wrong, but it's no good anymore. I don't even like coming home. We're both unhappy, and we were so happy when we got married. I'm dying to give you love and attention, but I need you to give me a chance. I'm not angry. I'm disappointed. I'm about ready to give up. If you want to end it, say so. If you don't, then, for God's sake, let's talk.

I know what I am. I'm an enabling codependent, whatever the hell that means. And you're an alcoholic, and I'm not really sure what that means. All I know is that I've been bailing you out for twenty-five years, and I'm sick and tired of doing it. But it's killing me. I'll tell you, one of these days when I get a call from that bar to come and get you, I'm going to start the car up in the garage and suck up the fumes.

I don't know if I did right or wrong, but I do know that I've done you no good. Anyway, I'm going to move in with my sister. She's been begging me to do so for years. The kids have been asking me to move in with her, too. They gave up on you years ago. I haven't got anyone else. But I haven't got you either, so what's the use of staying? Tonight, when you get drunk, at least you'll have a good excuse. If you ever want me back, call me after you've been sober for a year. I'll listen.

I try to talk to you, but you're never interested. I can't stand the TV anymore. Why don't you ever read a book? I'm starved for some good conversation. We've finally got time—the kids are gone, and I'm retired. You don't even try to understand what I'm about.

You say that my nose is always in a book. And you're right. And I say your nose is always in a TV program. So where are we? Not talking. I'll go anywhere with you that you want to go. We've got nothing but time; let's plan a vacation together. We can afford it.

My God, all you do is spend money. We're maxed out on plastic. When you go shopping, you go crazy. I can't stand going into our closet any more. It's too much.

Would you try something new? For a month, let's only go shopping together. I can work out the time, no problem. If we can't afford it, I'll tell you why. I'm not Ebenezer Scrooge. I hate seeing you unhappy. How about trying it?

As soon as I come in the door, you start nagging. "Why weren't you home earlier?" "The kids hardly see you." "The toilet's still running." I tell you, I hate coming home anymore.

I know you're dissatisfied. I'm dissatisfied, too. You keep nagging, I keep withdrawing. Where are we going? Is this the marriage you want? Let's get your mother to take care of the kids, so we can go away for a weekend and try to figure this thing out. I've given up caring who's right and who's wrong. I'd like some time to love you and to talk together. Anything would be better than this.

I wish to God you'd go back to work. I had a life when you were working. Now I have nothing. You poke your nose into everything I do, and then, if you don't approve, you tell me what I'm doing wrong or you give me the silent treatment. I'm still in business here; I haven't stopped running the house. Butt out and let me run my business.

All our marriage I never told you what to do unless you asked me. But you've always told me what to do. I didn't like it, but I've always had so many things to do it wasn't such a big deal as long as you were running your business. Well, I still have a lot of things to do. But now you're around all the time. It's stifling. So let's have a business meeting. I'm your biggest customer and I'm very dissatisfied. What would you do if you had an unhappy customer you didn't want to lose?

You said you'd call last night, but you didn't. You'd better have a damn good reason why.

It's so good to hear from you. What's happening? Any news about that contract you've been working on so hard?

Why are you so afraid of making a commitment? Our relationship is going nowhere! I'm tired of waiting for you to make up your mind. Marry me or I'm leaving.

Since we're spending the whole weekend together, I want to have a really good time. I've decided not to talk about our future. In fact, I'm not ever going to talk about it again. Ever! It's up to you. And I'm not going to nag or criticize you. I've just given up begging you to marry me. I haven't given up on getting married.

You're never home. It's work, work, work. Well it's work, work, work for me, too. Doris's husband is just like you. And she's asked me to go out. I don't want to, but I'm hungry for some love and attention from you. What the hell do I have to do to get some?

I understand you've got to work. I appreciate it that we have enough money to live the life we're living. But I'm lonely for you, for some fun, for something I'm not getting from this marriage. I want to talk and I want to make love. How about giving me Wednesday nights? I'll get a baby-sitter; we'll go out and be together. It's not for me and it's not for you; it's for our marriage.

Every year you get more and more like your father. Every time we're over there, I watch him go around winding up all the goddamn clocks. It drives me crazy. When they start chiming all at once, I'd like to smash every one of them. Now you've begun to buy clocks. Are you some kind of clone? Hey, I'm only fifty-six. If this is what I've got to look forward to, I'm out of here.

You say your dad called you all alarmed because I went over there with the video camera and took pictures of him all afternoon. I just told him to go about his business, that I was working on a documentary of what retirement's like. After that, he seemed to enjoy it; he never complained to me. Anyway the tape came out great. I want to show it to you. Why did I do it? I'll tell you, but I think you'll be able to figure it out. Your mother thought it was hysterical; she wants to show it to her bridge club.

TEACHER TO STUDENT

That does it! I told you to settle down and get to work. . . . Okay, you asked for it, no recess today.

Boys and girls, I'm going to play some more of the music you liked so much yesterday. As soon as it's over, let's settle down and go to work on our math. Remember, if you get stuck, just raise your hand and I'll come right over.

You copied this paper right off the Internet. You know the rule, you bought yourself an F on the whole unit.

You must have read a lot of papers on the Internet before you picked this one. I agree it really covers the subject. But I can't give you credit because you didn't write it. But look, I like it. If you'll write a paper and explain why this is a good one, I'll accept it. I don't want any of you to stop using the Internet. Anytime you want to copy something, just mention where you got it and do a good job of telling me why you think it was worth copying.

I'm sick and tired of having to watch you like a hawk whenever you take a test. The next time I catch any of you cheating, it's going in your permanent record and your parents are going to get a letter explaining why. Think about it.

Today's test is something new: only one question, but write no more than two pages to answer it; one would be better. If you don't like my question and can think of a better one, show it to me and I'll tell you if it's okay. You may use your book and your notes; you may even help each other. When you finish, come up to my desk and explain what you wrote. The minimum grade is a B, which means you really know the material. No C or D work is acceptable. If you have to take the test home tonight to get your B or raise it to an A, that's fine. If you like this way of testing, let's talk about it.

The next time you won't wait for your turn at tetherball, you're benched for a week.

I know you are having trouble waiting for your turn. Let's sit down here and talk while the others take their turns. You're really good, you know. How did you learn to play so well?

Starting tomorrow, I'm going to lock the door when the bell rings. If you're not in the room, go to the office, and you'll get an F for the day. If you don't go directly to the office and sit until your next class, you'll get Saturday detention.

I don't like the way kids who come to class late are being treated. I don't want to threaten you, and you have better things to do than sit in the office or detention on Saturdays. If you want to talk about what we could do that will get you here on time, I'm willing. You never complain about what we're doing in here; the way I see it is that you're just not used to getting to class on time. There's some really neat stuff coming up in this unit, and I'd hate to see any of you miss it.

There's too much hitting and fighting. If I catch any of you hitting anyone, I'm going to write your name on the board and call your mother. If you do it again, your mother is going to have to come to school and meet with the principal.

We're going to sit in a circle from now on. Everyone will be in the front row. This way, anytime you need me, I'll be right there to help out. See, my chair's on wheels, so I can scoot anywhere in the room in a second. I'm not looking for anyone to punish. All I want is for us to get along and enjoy learning. Since we're in a circle, let's begin today with a class meeting and get to know each other better.

You all groan when it's time for math. The next person I catch will really have something to groan about.

From now on, we're going to do math in teams of three. Each day we'll do two story problems that I'm going to take from one of the old state tests. Talk them over and do them. If you need my help, raise your hands. Every team has to tell me how they did the problems. When you think you've got the answers, raise your hands and I'll come over to your team. If the solutions aren't right, ask questions and then work until you get the problems right. There'll be no more failures, no low grades. Everybody will get all the questions right all the time.

You're doing a poor job on homework. I don't ask you to do much, but most of you don't do anything. From now on, your mother has to check your homework and sign it. If she doesn't have the time, find someone who can. If you miss five assignments, all you can get is a D. If you miss six, you fail. You've got to learn to be responsible.

Next week, I'm going to assign homework only when we don't finish what we're doing in class. If you all buckle down, you shouldn't have to do much at home. But if you want a good grade, take your work home and do something to make it better. Let's talk about this plan in our circle every day for a few minutes to see how it's going.

Any student who is caught smoking on school property will be automatically suspended for three days and given an F in all his or her classes for those three days.

Instead of suspension, any student who is caught smoking the first time will be given an opportunity to tell the counselor what he or she does or wants to do for fun. Our job will be to try to figure out how students can have more fun in school safely. If students can have more safe fun, we think they will choose to smoke less. This is a school problem. If you want to start meeting to figure out a solution, we'll work with all who are interested.

If you get any further behind, you're going to flunk.

You're way behind. Let's forget about what you've failed so far and try to get you going on what you'll need to do for promotion to high school. Simply do the work, show me you know it, and you'll make it to high school. We've still got three months; you have time. I'm on your side, so use my help.

I'll tell you, John, you're going to have to sit by yourself the rest of the year. Stop bothering everybody around you.

CHOICE THEORY ALTERNATIVE

I'm tired of punishing you, John. I want to be your friend. I think you need some friends. I have time this afternoon during my free period to talk with you about making friends. I'd like to get to know you better.

Stop pushing and arguing with each other! If I have to keep you in for recess the rest of the year, it's okay with me. I hope you all like third grade because almost all of you are going to be back here next year.

I'm going to begin to teach you something new. It explains why you're happy when you're happy and sad when you're sad. You can use it to figure out how to be happier than you are now. It's a lot of fun. Let's put all the other work aside and do a new lesson for the rest of the day. A half hour is plenty of time to get started learning choice theory.

Starting tomorrow, I'm calling the truant officer about everyone who misses school without a legitimate excuse.

I'm not sure why so many of you are absent, but we have a rule: Too many unexcused absences mean you fail. Some of you are very close to that. I'd like to try something that may help. I need a committee of students to talk to those who were absent the the day before and ask them to come to school—just call them up the next morning and tell them they're missed here. I think it will help. Who will agree to make the calls? I need about five volunteers.

MANAGER TO EMPLOYEE

The company's installing Deming's new management system. His most important point is: Drive out fear. So my job is to ask you if there is anything you fear around here. For example, how about me? Are you afraid of me?

The company is installing Deming's new management system. His most important point is: Drive out fear. They want me to ask everyone in my group if you're afraid of anything. How anyone can answer that question honestly in this company is beyond me. But I'll tell you, I think you're doing a good job. I guess I don't tell you that enough. If you can be of any help to me in what they want me to do, I'd appreciate it if we could talk about it.

I guess it's time for your annual evaluation. This is what I've written down. I don't think we need to take very long. But there a few things I think you could improve.

I'm not putting you through the farce of our annual evaluation. I've reduced it to four questions that I think are easy to answer. I want you to tell me what you do around here that you think is really good—something you're proud of. Next, I'd like you to tell me something that you'd like to improve. Then, would you be willing to share your expertise with any of the people who are trying to improve in your strong area? And would you be willing to talk to one of the people who has had a lot of success in the area in which you want to improve? That's all.

We're trying hard to become a quality school. But every time I walk by your door, all the kids seem to be doing is having fun. I know fun is a basic need, but I think you're pushing it too far.

I tell you, it's no fun to be a principal. And then I walk by your room, and you and the kids seem to be having so much fun. Would it be too much to ask if I could visit your class and see how you do it? You seem to be doing something what's very hard to do. Take me, for instance; I haven't yet figured out how to have fun as a principal. I wonder if I could ask your kids that question. But look, I don't want to be a wet blanket. If you think you or your kids will be uncomfortable, I won't come.

I'm under pressure from the new owners to cut expenses. I've got to cut two more people. But if you get cut, I don't want you to take it personally.

I'm under pressure from the new owners to cut expenses. They say I have to cut two more people. I don't have any idea how to do it. As far as I can see, we're doing the same job now that we did before the last cut. I'm talking to each one of you individually. What I want is anything you can think of that might allow me to avoid cutting anyone. I want to have a meeting with all of you and invite my boss to attend. I want us to present to him all we're now doing and possibly could do to cut costs. The way I see it, it's our only chance.

Okay, this is the last time. If you screw up one more time, you're out of here. If you want to resign today, you'll have a better record than if we have to let you go.

I won't protect you anymore. You used to be the top salesman in the group. All we get now is orders from your old customers, and even they're complaining that you don't follow through. I'll tell you what I think: It's alcohol. We can help you with that problem. If it isn't alcohol, then tell me what it is. Don't look so shocked. This is an emergency. The only way I can save your job is if you go into treatment today. Your wife will be here in a few minutes; her mother is bringing her. A security man will drive you to the treatment center. Call me anything you want; all I hear now is the alcohol talking.

I know you're very uncomfortable with the quality school ideas. I'm uncomfortable, too. But I was told to do it, and this is the way it's going to be.

We're trying to become a quality school, so everything I'm trying to do is based on one principle. If I do this or I do that, will you (the staff) and I get closer together and more supportive of each other or further apart and less supportive? I'm not going to change anything unless you say it's okay.

I keep sending kids to the office, but nothing happens. What good is a principal who won't support us?

I'm very uncomfortable with this new no-punishment system. I'm trying my best to figure out what's going on. I send a kid to the office, and when I ask him what happened, and he says "nothing." But he seems to have gotten some help. Could I come to the office for a few days during my free period to see you work with the kids? Things seem to be getting better in this school, and I'm trying to figure out why.

Sales are down. There's nothing wrong with our product, so it's something you're doing or not doing. I think you've had it too easy. You've lost your hustle. I'd advise all of you to get going and bring in some better figures this month. Any questions?

I guess we've had so many good years that I've gotten complacent. I used to do a lot of things that I don't do anymore. I don't want to be a pain, but I want to get a little more active: make some calls with you and sit down and figure out some new strategy. If I'm off base, tell me. Things could be better; maybe our product is not as competitive as it used to be. Let's not make this a big deal. I really could care less whose fault it is. I just want to do my part to solve the problem.

I don't have an easy job. There were three people up for the promotion, and I picked someone else. No, I can't guarantee that you'll get the next opening. I can't guarantee anything. I don't have to explain it to you. You wouldn't agree with me anyway.

Why did I pick Harry instead of you or Bob? That's a question I had to answer for my boss. And it was hard enough. But to answer it for you is impossible. There's nothing I can say that would satisfy either of you. You don't feel very good about me now, and the more I try to make you understand, the more you'll dislike me. But unless you're planning to leave, we've got to work together. You do a great job, and I need you in that job. You have a right to be upset, and I have a right to continue to treat you as well as I can. If there is anything else I can do outside of the promotion, please let me know.

I know I'm twenty years younger than you. And I know I've only been here for three years and you've been here for thirty. But I'm your boss and I expect you to treat me as if I am. I want you at all the meetings just like everyone else. And on time.

This is a tough situation. I'm your boss, and I'm younger than your oldest son. Computers have changed everything. You know that as well as I do. But there's only so much computers can do. They know a billion things, but they have no wisdom or experience. You've got both. You can help me if you want to. I'll listen to you.

CONCLUSION

It takes time to learn to use a new language that is different from what has been used on you all your life and that you began using when you were very young. If you want to learn the language of choice theory, I suggest that you start paying attention to what you say and how you say it with everyone, even strangers. Getting along better with everyone you encounter is to both your and their advantage. Even if people you are talking to use external control language, try to respond with choice theory. You will find that most people are intrigued. It is not that people are against using choice theory, it is that most of them don't even know it exists. If you find this book useful and haven't read the 1998 book, *Choice Theory: A New Psychology of Personal Freedom,* we strongly urge you to do so. There is a lot to learn if you want to put this theory to work in every part of your life.

ABOUT THE WILLIAM GLASSER INSTITUTE

The William Glasser Institute teaches choice theory, reality therapy, and quality management all over the world. More than five thousand counselors of both adults and children, teachers, school administrators, and managers of other organizations have gone through the Institute Certification Program, and many more are in the training process. Dr. Glasser's latest interest is in teaching these ideas to entire communities using his 1998 book, *Choice Theory*, as the text. Institute instructors are located all over the United States and Canada, as well as in many other countries of the world. Training by local instructors is available on site or close to where most people live. Videotapes of Dr. Glasser counseling and a variety of other materials are also available. For further information, contact: The William Glasser Institute, 22024 Lassen Street, Suite 118, Chatsworth, CA 91311; phone: 818-700-8000; fax: 818-700-0555.